ISBN 978-1-332-85406-6
PIBN 10228826

1 MONTH OF
FREE
READING

at

www.ForgottenBooks.com

By purchasing this book you are eligible for one month membership to ForgottenBooks.com, giving you unlimited access to our entire collection of over 1,000,000 titles via our web site and mobile apps.

To claim your free month visit:

www.forgottenbooks.com/free228826

The
Memory Book

Wherein the members
of the
Illinois Woman's
Press Association
have written bits of
feminine philosophy
and fancy, and
wherein you may
write your own

In collecting and editing this material, I
make sincere acknowledgments to my
committee: Idah McGlone Gibson, Page
Waller Eaton, Caroline A. Huling and
Violet Moore Higgins for their help and
encouragement. To them is due what-
ever success this volume merits.

Elizabeth Curtiss Nolan
Chairman

Foreword

THE Memory Book is finished and what shall I say as a foreword?

Suggestions come in battalions, and verily the memories of "ye olden times" should be most precious to all who con its pages.

The marvel of memory makes of life the real high and holy thing it is—a bond between the past and present—the prelude of the future. Memory is that function of the brain which is most essential in the education and development of humanity. Without memory reasoning would fail, since one must remember premises in order to discuss rationally any grave theme of business, politics, home, literature. Aye! even happiness will be nil if one remembers not love.

Maeterlinck denies the immortality of memory, depending, as it does, for expression upon the brain function—the brain necessarily dying with the rest of the body. Hence, while granting the immortality of the soul, he denies that we shall know each other when spirit reveals itself to spirit.

Those of us with old-fashioned church training ask such immortality as shall conduce to the growth of the individual soul, which, we believe, will mean happiness. Verily such development cannot continue without the consciousness of kinship of soul and the renewal of the loves of this life. This, memory alone can give.

Grave thoughts hark back to the storehouse of Illinois Woman's Press Association memories, and over the bridge from the then of eighteen eighty-six to the now of nineteen fourteen come pleasant recollections of the long ago, and I am glad to realize that the founders of the Illinois Woman's Press Association, which now is a power in the state, were women of force— of gracious bearing—of fine culture and refinement—of broad outlook on human affairs.

Over the Bridge of Memories come trooping a host of dear and familiar figures; Mrs. Conant, daring in enterprise and earnest of purpose, though frail of physique, who led in the establishment of our organization; Frances Willard and Mary Allen West, devotees of a noble cause, who spent brain and physical force for the promotion of temperance; Dr. Stevenson, loyal, scholarly, and clever with the pen; Eliza Bowman, devoted altruist, who gave of her mother-love to the homeless waifs of the street; Rosa Miller Avery, earnest worker for the ballot for women before the idea had become quite the fashion; Mrs. Robert C. Clowry, who believed in woman's suffrage, and *was, it is said, the first American woman to write and publish an opera.* . . .

I will say no more, yet I trow all members of the Illinois Woman's Press Association can recall a long list of earnest, cultivated women who have made the Association what it is, and have made the world better for their being in it.

There is a hidden chamber in each heart where memory keeps its precious things, and sometimes in the quiet eventime, I pray my readers steal away for a little while and call up the memories of Auld Lang Syne.

We women of the Press Association are friends with all which that name implies. We do not treat our friendship "daintily," but with courage—we have truth to the other. We even think aloud in our meetings, ready to share the give and take of disputation—seasoned as it always is with generous appreciation—and truly out of these experiences of life do grow the characters which are forceful factors in civic and literary life!

From this atmosphere we are sending out our book. The "leif motif" of the scheme is love. The variations are made according to the trend of individual effort, this scheme being an outgrowth of the spirit which dominated the formation of the organization.

Each for all and all for each is the thought of the members, and our hope is that The Memory Book may reach the inner chamber of many hearts.

An old Spanish proverb runs in this wise: "Let Providence manage never so fairly, someone is displeased." Job in his protest against the unwisdom of his sympathizing friends, who so sorely tried his soul, exclaimed at the end of his patience, "Oh! that mine adversary would write a book!" Can one guess the tone of his contemplated review? What a commentary upon human nature! Even Providence does not go unchallenged!

What an outlook for the daring members of the Illinois Woman's Press Association!

Julia Holmes Smith, M. D.

A Psalm of Womanhood

By Belle Squire

AS Woman my dignity is supreme, for I am sculptress of the race, the architect of humanity. My body is the Temple, the Holy of Holies, wherein are fashioned into indelible shape, for weal or woe, the children who are to come. Therefore must I keep my temple pure and clean, nor ever let it be defiled by thought or word or deed, for within me lies, mayhap, the destiny of millions yet unborn.

At its peril will the race defile me, stunt me, hinder me in my high calling, for outraged Nature will herself avenge my wrong, and demand in full the penalty for my hurt. I can not fall alone, the race will suffer with me, for its destiny is bound up within mine own. I am indeed supreme, for I am a Woman!

My part is difficult, but I will not flinch. I must be strong as the oak on the bleakest hill, and tender and sweet and pure as the flower that blooms in the valley below 🌿 🌿

I am the citadel that must never capitulate, nor must I be taken unawares. Until Death o'ercomes me I must be mistress of myself, for I am Woman and must be free, or the race will be carried into that captivity from which there is no return.

Being Woman, a vital part of Humanity itself, I must demand and use, if need be, every human right that belongs to Humanity, be it civil, moral, industrial or political, for I am half the race. I am Woman. For Freedom's sake I must be free, for I am sculptress, architect of Humanity, its citadel, its oak, its blossom. I am Woman, Mother and Molder of the Race!

Noblesse Oblige

IF I am weak and you are strong
   Why then, why then
     To you the braver deeds belong.
      And so again,
If you have gifts and I have none,
If I have shade and you have sun,
    'Tis yours with freer hand to give,
    'Tis yours with truer grace to live,
Than I who giftless, sunless, stand,
With barren life and hand.

We do not ask the little brook
  To turn the wheel;
Unto the larger stream we look.
  The strength of steel
We do not ask from silken band,
Nor heart of oak from willow wand;
    We do not ask the wren to go
    Up to the heights the eagles know;
Nor yet expect the lark's clear note,
From out the dove's dumb throat.

'Tis wisdom's law, the perfect code,
  By love inspired;
Of him on whom much is bestowed,
  Is much required;
The tuneful throat is bid to sing,
The oak must reign the forest's king,
    The rushing stream the wheel must move,
    The tempered steel its strength must prove,
'Tis given unto the eagle's eyes
To face the mid-day skies.

Carlotta Perry

It Will Be Better Tomorrow

IT IS not wise to make a magnet of one's thoughts to attract trouble. Let us anticipate happiness. Let us expect success. Let us believe that all the good things which we hope for and pray for and work for have started our way. They may be some time in coming, and perhaps they will not come in exactly the manner that we had mapped out, but if we keep our courage and do our duty our hopes will be realized.

Thoughts are vital. We help or hinder our purposes by the quality of the thought which we bring to our daily task. We are what we think we are. We can accomplish just what we think we can. If we honestly believe we cannot accomplish a certain task we may as well give it up while that belief lasts.

The remedy is to get out of such a belief. Get out of the atmosphere of doubt and distrust. Get into the current of Faith. Adopt the creed of Courage and Good Cheer.

"It will be better tomorrow," was the motto of a brave little woman who waited through many tomorrows for the good fortune that finally came; and it is a good motto for all of us.

Optimism is a powerful lever for lifting a trouble. The woman who can keep a hopeful view and a smiling face while she copes with a difficulty has conquered it already.

The successful people are those who have learned the art of transforming difficulties into working power. The happy people are those who have learned that the joy of living comes from trying to make others happy. Neither success nor happiness ever comes from anticipating trouble.

Mate Palmer.

Some Definitions

GOD—

God to each person is what he, in his inmost soul, feels that he himself should be. To be "Godlike" is partially to attain that ideal.

PRAYER—

Prayer is the ladder on which the human soul exalts itself to view the Infinite.

LOVE—

"Greater love hath no man than this that a man lay down his life for his friends." How many among us would stand that test?

FRIENDS—

We know not who they are until their friendship is tested. Though many are called few are chosen.

MEMORY—

A faculty that ofttimes brings more pain than pleasure; yet who would be without it?

Caroline A. Huling.

After Glow

INTO the maze and darkness of my life—you came!
Straightway the sun arose and glorified the way.
Now you are gone—I journey faltering as before,
But through the darkness shines the radiance of the vanished
day.

Page Waller Eaton.

MY FAIRYLAND

CARO SENOUR

1. My Fair - y-land, My Fair - y-land, I love the days of Fair - y-land, Where
2. My Fair - y-land, My Fair - y-land, I love the days of Fair - y-land, Where
3. My Fair - y-land, My Fair - y-land, I love the days of Fair - y-land, Where
4. My Fair - y-land, My Fair - y-land, I love the days of Fair - y-land, The

wea - ry heads ne'er toss a-round, And tir - ed feet can al-ways bound; Where merry voices
fair - ies dance and sing for me, And can-dy grows on ev-'ry tree; Where birds dress in their
chil-dren romp and kit - tens play, And dog-gies dance and dol-lies gay, Join with the fair-ies
train leaves at the time, you know, When gowns and nightcaps are the go, When choo choo whistles

form a band, In my sweet home, my Fair - y-land.
col - ors grand, In my sweet home, my Fair - y-land.
hand in hand, In my sweet home, my Fair - y-land.
blow, you land In my sweet home, my Fair - y-land.

Mirandy on Fame

"YOU ain't got 'bout a dollar an' a half layin' around loose dat you could advance me on nex' week's washin'?" inquired Mirandy, with a shamed-faced air.

"I hates to borror, for hit sho'ly does make you tired to have to work for money dat you done already spent, but whut wid de Sons of Zion presentin' Ike wid a lovin' cup, and Thomas Jefferson bein' 'lected de President of de Black and Tan Football Club, an' Ma'y Jane bein' pinted de Queen of Sheba at de Sunday School blowout de famb'ly puss look lak a elephant done trod on hit.

"Yassum, we all is gittin' famous, an' fame suttinly do come high. I done took notice befo' dis dat all dem folks whut is got dey statues an' dey pictures up in de parks an' de public places has got a mighty lean an' hungry 'pearance, an' I knows de reason now dat dey is so peeked-lookin'—dey had to spend so much money on dey halos dat dey didn't have no change left to buy corn beef an' cabbage.

"Yassum, hit sho'ly am expensive to be distinctious, an' ef dere hadn't been one po', humble, ordinary woman in our house to keep de pot a bilin' I 'specks I could name de name of two favorite sons an' a daughter dat was mighty puffed up wid pride, but dat wouldn't a had nothin' else to stay deir stomachs on but compliments.

"An' compliments is lak dried apples—dey is sweet, an' tasty, an' dey swells you all up, but dey is all wind—all wind. Dey don't stand by lak pork chops.

"Dey got to live up to deir reputation, an' hit costs mo' to support a reputation dan hit does a pair of twins.

"Now dere's Ike. Ike is de most popularest man in de church, an' de union, an' whenever anybody comes along an' starts up a new 'sciety hits foreordained an' predestinated, as Brer Jenkins would say, dat Ike is gwine to be 'lected wid a risin' vote to be de president, or de secretary, or de cheerman of de finance committee, or somethin' or nother dats got a fourteen hour day wuk in hit an' no pay.

"Cose hit seems mighty grand to be dat prominent, an' ev'y time dey saddles him wid a new honor, an' mo' wuk, Ike comes home wid his chest stickin' out so far dat he busts his shirt buttons off, an' I goes out de next mawnin' an' hunts up another job of washin'.

"Yassum, dere used to be some interest in de days when Ike was onknown, in lookin' farward to Saturday night when he got his pay envelope, but now by de time he gits through headin' de contribution list becaze he is de treasurer, an' losin' a day's wuk becaze, bein' de president of de organization, he has to 'tend de funerals, an' ride wid de mourners when a member dies, dere ain't enough left to make it wuth de trouble to go through his pocket arfter he goes to sleep.

"You see hit was lak dis—de odder night Ike come home a-grinnin' from year to year, an' wid a mighty uplifted look on his face, an' he says to me as I was a gittin' supper:

" 'Mirandy, dis am a proud day for you, an' you ought to be a thankful woman dat you married lak you did.'

" 'Ef I is ever out-married myself, I ain't never found hit out,' 'sponds I, for it don't do to let on to your husband dat you think too well of him. Nawn, hit makes him too uppity. 'But whuts de matter now?' I axes.

" 'De Sons of Zion,' says Ike, a-puffin' hisself up, 'is gwine to present me wid a lovin' cup as a slight testimonial of deir esteem, an' of de noble an' conscientious way in which I is done my duty.'

" 'Humph,' says I; 'dey gives you de mug, but I lay we'se got to fill hit.'

" 'Of course,' 'spons Ike in a high an' mighty tone, 'we can do no less to show our appreciation of de honor dat is been done me.'

"Well, dat night a committee of de brethren come 'round to present de lovin' cup.

"Yassum, an' befo' dat night was over dat chany mug dat you could a bought in de store for thirty-five cents, done cost us three dollars an' fifty cents in beer, let lone de war an' tar on de furniture dat come arfter de lovin' cup is been around 'bout six times, an' two of de brethren got mixed up in a little argyment 'bout whether Ike was a greater man dan Napoleon.

"Yassum, glory suttinly does come high. Fame is somethin' dat you spend your life wurkin' for—an' den hit lands you in de po' house."

Dorothy Dix.

A Memory Page

I WONDER IS THERE LAUGHTER

I · WONDER
   VP · IN · HEAVEN
     IS · THERE · LAVGHTER
FOR · HER · WHO · LOVED · IT · SO,
IF, · PARTING · PAST, · THE · JOY
    THAT · FOLLOWED · AFTER
MADE · HER · LESS · LOATH · TO · GO?
I · WONDER · IF · BEYOND · THE
     STARS' · STRANGE · SINGING,
THE · HIGH · ANGELIC · PRAISE,
SHE · HEARS · THOSE · NOTES · OF · VA-
    GRANT · LAVGHTER · RINGING
THAT · GLADDENED · EARTHLY
               DAYS ?

I · WONDER · IF · THIS · LITTLE
    LIFE · BEHIND · HER,
ETERNITY · BEFORE,
SOME · TENDER · THOVGHT · OF · JOY
    AND · MIRTH · MIGHT · FIND
             HER
FROM · ONE · WHO · LAVGHS · NO
           MORE: -
IT · MATTERS · NOT, · MY · LONELI-
    NESS, · MY · SORROW,
SO · SHE · BE · GLAD · AND · GAY -
BVT · IF · I · THOVGHT · SHE · WOVLD
    NOT · LAVGH · TOMORROW
MY · HEART · WOVLD
    BREAK · TODAY!

Fred M. Colson

Rosemary for Remembrance

WHO does not know the power of fragrance to bring back or awaken memories of the past?

How subtle the perfume of the lilac, the wild rose, the primrose of the English hedgerow, and the honeysuckle over the cottage door!

What memories cling and cluster around them when, after a long interval of time, their delicate odor is wafted to us!

Rosemary for remembrance! Just a whiff is enough to carry us back to scenes and times long since past. Do we forget? Are our dear ones lost to us? No, we do not forget and our friends are with us in memory. The noble, lovable women we have known, during the lifetime of the I. W. P. A. come out from the mists which have obscured them, and we, for a moment, behold them more lovely and lovable than when we beheld them in the flesh.

A Shakespeare garden is a real, tangible thing; in it are still planted the various herbs mentioned in the dramas. In memory's garden we find the sweet smelling carnation which holds and occupies a sunny place, and its perfume brings to us tender thoughts of days long since past, of noble deeds well done. Let us be grateful for every sweet flower that blooms and cultivate Rosemary for Remembrance.

Mary A. Ahrens.

To My Mother

IF WE can bring to the lives of our friends but a meagre portion of the joy and devotion showered upon us by our parents, we shall not have lived in vain.

Rose D. Meyer.

Color

GOD'S truth may fall upon our souls, just as a shaft
    of light,
    Whose oft-seen dazzling radiance escapes our sight
Until a prism severs it and lo! a heavenly rainbow shade—
  And through that melody of color there's a misty image
    made.

Then one espies some red and cries: "I see the Light!
    Red heralds courage, force, and physical delight!
Find fun in Now and fume not at Tomorrow's flight,
    Just be a Hedonist and laugh at any plight!"

Another yellow sees; its beams bewitch his eye,
    To him it means "There is but Soul and Soul is I.
There is no red, there is no blue, for Soul embraces all;
    God's Truth in yellow gleams. Oh! heed the Spirit's call!"

A third from out the darkness calls: "I have found blue,
    The color of the Intellect, of Science, of the True.
There is but Mind. The soul's a myth, for blue means Mind!"
    Thus cults begin for those who think they know and are
    so blind.

A fourth's enchanted by the rainbow's subtle call,
    And gazes like a Hindoo at a crystal ball,
Until, forsooth, he purple finds, and is enwrapped in awe;
    And he a mystic is, and cobwebs paths to God's Truth-law.

Yet that pure shaft of Light illumes the world and gives it life,
    While our poor vision sees but green or gray and makes no
    strife
For ultra-violet and infra-red beyond the spectrum's scope;
    But live content to see one tint and leave the rest to Hope.

God grant our race may gain the virile force that is the red,
    The blue-flamed torch of thought by which we may be led,
The inspiration of the Radiance so yellow bright,
    And Love that blendeth all, and grows to know the Perfect
    Light.

Myrtle Dean Clark.

At Horace Greeley's Home

THE Editor-farmer went to Chappaqua, his home, the evening before, and his smiling face met the visitors who came in the first morning train from New York City. Guests were flocking in throughout the day.

The first act was a social stroll over the farm. The Blonde Philosopher led the way, and pointed out where we could find the rarest apples. The large old farmhouse proper was soon in view—"The pleasantest spot on the place to live in, if Mrs. Greeley would ever consent to have about an acre of trees cut down; but she cannot make up her mind to that."

After we had seen Mr. Greeley's special spring, one of several which feed a creek that meanders around mossy rocks, and we had followed the winding of a road under a variety of shady trees, we came to his "model barn." There the next President of the United States seated himself on a rock with the ladies, and used this first opportunity to look into the daily newspapers, while the men scattered on an independent stroll and smoke.

In the house the daughter, Miss Ida, was the cordial hostess. The younger sister, Miss Gabrielle, is a cherry-cheeked, rosy-lipped, white-toothed maiden of "sweet sixteen's" artlessness. After dinner, the ladies played croquet, and in her room lay the invalid, Mrs. Greeley, wide-awaake and strong in mind. Her frankly spoken, impressive thoughts, we shall always remember.

While Mr. Greeley dozed over the Tribune, the men discussed politics rapidly; until the Philosopher, startled from his nap exclaimed: "Oh! Mr. S., you mustn't get out of temper!" "But such lies!"—The Sage replied: "If you expect a presidential election without lies, you may as well expect a Summer without grasshoppers."

By the afternoon train we all returned, and to this day in far-off Nineteen Hundred and Fourteen, I remember that I was the privileged one to be seated by the great and genial editor, until at New York City a friend and closed carriage smuggled him away from curious eyes.

A few weeks later Horace Greeley and Mrs. Greeley were breathing the ether of The Better Land.

(Condensed from Anna Ballard's report in the next day's New York Sunday Mercury, September eighth, eighteen seventy-two.)

Anna Ballard.

The Dunes

HERE Nature sings her quaintest tunes,
    And dons her dearest robes of fairy
      Among the sandy, wind-swept dunes,

And to the listening reeds she croons
A cradle song elf-like and airy,—
Here Nature sings her quaintest tunes,

And if you walk 'neath Autumn moons
Of wraith-like forms you'd best be wary,
Among the sandy, wind-swept dunes;

For Hecote chants her mystic runes
To charm us into paths contrary,—
Here Nature sings her quaintest tunes,

And to the weary brings her boons
Of rest and pleasures salutary
Among the sandy, wind-swept dunes.

So here, on fading afternoons,
I wander, lost in sweet vagary;
Here Nature sings her quaintest tunes,
Among the sandy, wind-swept dunes.

Florence Holbrook.

I Watched the Children

I WATCHED the children playing in the sunlight,
    The children with their wind-blown locks astray,
    The children with their wind-kissed eager faces,
The merry, merry children at their play.

Ah, very young and careless are the children,
    Ah, very old and tired my heart today.
So long ago it is, do I remember?—
    I joined the merry children at their play.

Leonora Pease.

A Memory Page

A Prayer for Every Day

O Thou, Almighty Power!
Teach me to take from Thee my dole
Of good or ill, and murmur not.
O, make my finite mind to grasp
That, in Thy infinite plan, there is
No place for my weak cries against
The grief and sorrow of the common
    lot.
Blot out the Ego that doth crush my
    soul
Beneath its load of selfishness and
    greed,
And let me know, what now I dimly
    guess,
The fullness of Thy purposes, for my
    desire
For which I vainly plead, when
    placed beside
Humanity's great need, sinks into
    nothingness.
Oh Thou, High Over All!
Suffer my mean, ungenerous prayer,
That Thou wouldst change Thy
    changeless laws,
Which make strict justice, mercy
    most divine,
To fall on unheeding ears. Bring me
To feel Thy love, which, all em-
    bracing, wraps
Not only me about, but takes the
    whole
Great universe within its sheltering
    folds.
Thy way is right; and though in fol-
    lowing it
My path leads o'er the plowshare's
    lurid red,
Still will I trust Thy guidance sure,
    and say
While yet I lift my streaming eyes
    to Thee,
Thy will be done.

        Idah McGlone Gibson.

The Legend of the Seven Corn Maidens

WE ARE a people who run after strange gods, and are more familiar with the story of the Pleiades than with the Indian legend of the seven lovely Corn Maidens.

This same legend is found among the Zunis of today and among the old Peruvians of a thousand years ago.

The Corn, so the legends tell, was created in the night and in the firelight. The seven Corn Maidens were seven stars from Heaven and they wished to create something which would be of benefit to the children of earth. So they formed a circle and danced about a sprig of grass.

They were joined in the dance by the Spirit of the Waters, who was a beautiful youth. They danced toward him, two by two, the eldest first, whilst the great Mother stood near, blessing. As their finger-tips touched his, fruit is given to the grass plant, and corn is created! But the grass still keeps its identity, as may be seen by the tassel at the top.

This was at night, and the ears of corn take their color from the firelight in which they were born.

When the fire is first lighted it gives a strong yellow flame. The first ear is yellow and signifies the North.

The red tip of the blaze gives the red ear, the South.

The intense blue flame gives the blue ear, the West; and as the fire dies down to white ashes, the white ears, the East—the Dawn!

When one blows upon the flames the sparks fly upward and the speckled ear is formed, which typifies the Upper Region.

Now all dies out and is black; we have the black ear—the Lower Regions.

Then, the sweet corn—the Virgin!

Great ceremonials are used in the winter when preparing the corn for planting. In religious rites, a large basket tray is used, around the outer edge of which is ranged the ears of seven colors. Next these are cakes, each carefully prepared from the separate colored ears, and in the center one of each of these cakes is taken and crumbled to pieces, typifying the final commingling of all into one great whole.

Legends of the Corn Maidens are endless.

This one was given by a priest of the Zuni.

Susan S. Frackleton.

The Fruit Tree

ONE fruit-tree in my little garden lives—
    White, white it stands!
    Celestial promise of the time it gives
Its fruits to arid lands.
But oh! my gratitude I may not write
    Till calmer hours;
So wonderful the perfect, present sight,
    God's gift of flowers!

Frances Squire Potter.

The Inner Silence

NOISES that strive to tear
    Earth's mantle soft of air
    And break upon the stillness where it dwells:
The noise of battle and the noise of prayer,
The cooing noise of love that softly tells
Joy's brevity, the brazen noise of laughter—
All these affront me not, nor echo after
    Through the long memories.
They may not enter the deep chamber where
    Forever silence is.

Silence more soft than spring hides in the ground
    Beneath her budding flowers;
Silence more rich than ever was the sound
    Of harps through long warm hours.
'Tis like a hidden vastness, even as though
Great suns might there beat out their measures slow
    Nor break the hush mightier than they.
    There do I dwell eternally,
    There where no thought may follow me.
Nor stillest dreams whose pinions plume the way.

Harriet Monroe.

COMPENSATION

MEDIUM

Words by M. H.

Music by
CARRIE JACOBS-BOND

Compensation (M)-2

The Real Fountain of Youth

THE Scotch soldier-preacher says: "We all get what we gang in for."

Take this for the watchword in the battle we are waging to keep young and vigorous so long as we all shall live.

Most of us have grown tired of the growing-old habit— we are all girls and boys of varying ages, and each day are more and more astonished to find how like ourselves everybody else is—all thinking of the difficulties and perplexities of growing old, weary of the process and wondering if there be any method for avoiding it.

In outward form people have stopped growing old. Men no longer tolerate long beards, women have ceased to don shoulder shawls and caps. The deaf no longer put hands behind the ear to hear, or before them like the Dutchman, to beg, "A little louder, please." Modern men and women fight the tendency to stoop, to use a cane. They wear rimless glasses, make regular visits to the dentist, breathe deeply, take cold baths, and sleep with open windows. By exercise they fight off double chins and too solid flesh.

I know a vigorous lady of eighty who talks of vaulting lightly into bed—and does it; another who, when she hears a hurdy-gurdy outside her window, cuts flying pigeon wings all 'round the room.

Conserving the activity of the brain cells, we give light to the eye, suppleness to the body, and remove to a distance illness, age—even death itself.

Why are actresses the youngest women in the land today? Because every faculty of body and mind is in constant use. They must be pointed, animated, alert, to the very last.

The surest way to keep young is to mingle with young people and persons of optimistic temperament. Cultivate their point of view, read wholesome books, frown down lugubrious recitals, refuse to brood over life's tragedies. Nothing mars the human visage so swiftly as fretfulness and complaining.

Study the problems which bring all the intellectual energies into use. Howells warns us of the danger, one day in middle life, when we slump and let a feeble performance blight the fame of strenuous endeavor.

Do not let go your hold on work. It is the only saving grace. Only through the great and constant blessing of endless endeavor will one find the spring for which Ponce de Leon vainly sought.

Helen Reynolds Kellogg, M. D.

When Daylight Fades

WHEN daylight fades
A silence broodeth over all the land;
The waves creep slowly up the glistening sand;
The roistering wind grows strangely still;
More sweetly sounds the music of the rill
When daylight fades.

When daylight fades
Long shadows gather on the pine crowned hill;
The mossy wheel turns slowly at the mill;
The downy chickens seek their mother's wing;
The crickets in the long lush grasses sing
When daylight fades.

When daylight fades
The whip-poor-will pipes forth his lonely call;
The dewdrops glisten on the old stone wall,
And sunset skies turn dim and faintly gray,
While fireflies flash their lamps across the way,
When daylight fades.

When daylight fades
The flowers drooping, nestle in their beds,
And babies, nodding curly, drowsy heads,
Are pillowed on their loving mothers' breast;
All living things are touched to tender rest,
When daylight fades.

When daylight fades
Into death's dreamless lethe-dipped starless night,
What fields elysian touched with unknown light;
What sun-kissed arching azure summer skies,
What flower-gemmed world will greet our waking eyes
When daylight fades?

Agnes Potter McGee.

Our Intellectual Life

COMPARATIVELY speaking, very few people in these days lead, in even a small degree, what may be called "the intellectual life." Men in business find, for the most part, that business practically absorbs their entire mental force; at the end of the day most men seek recreation in some other form than that which calls for brain-activity. Here and there are men who find rest in their libraries, reading "something good," or who are able to produce and enjoy music, but such men are apt to be "solitary;" their reading and thought, their recreation after toil, no matter upon what high plane it may be, is apt to be purely academic; such men are more in need of the stimulation of intellectual human companionship than of books; and that is the very thing they find hardest to get. Women, as a rule, find the cares of the household, or of business, if such is their lot, enough to absorb their nervous forces to such an extent that they are not equal to more intellectual exertion than is required by the game of bridge, or the mild demands of one of the late novels, or the current magazines. And yet, just why these individual units of intellectual activity should stagnate from the lack of stimulation of mental contact is indeed a weighty problem to solve.

We are either intellectually tired, or intellectually lazy, after business all day; one needs more recreation than an evening in his library; that form of intellectual exercise isn't vital and invigorating — we need to come more in contact with other minds than we can do by books. Academic reading is all right—but it ought to lead to practical uses; and it cannot and does not—without the personal element of association directly with other minds. It remains then to ask—can people, as a whole, be co-ordinated? And how may it be done?

Clever people are often individualists who make demands which other clever people fail to appreciate, and one hesitates in preparing a thesis on an abstract point like—"Can a man think in any century but his own?" The discussion is apt to become personal, and acrimonious. In these modern times, intellectual snobbishness always seems to underlie an intellectual uplift movement. If a man does not care for reflections of life interpreted through the medium of tone or color or poetic line, let him enjoy life at first hand; after all he may be saner than we.

Sadie E. Carver.

To the Men

JEST suppose you had to court by screechin' like a screech
  owl,
   Or else were forced to win your love by preenin' like a
    peafowl!
What if you had to slink an' dodge, like an old black vulture,
While you proved to your dear girl, your boundless love an'
  culture!
How would you like to woo her, by a heron's dancin',
Or as a courtin' pheasant does, a drummin' an' a prancin'!
Perhaps you'd have to sing to her, like a night hawk screechin',
Or imitate a vireo, turnin' somersaults an' preachin'!
Suppose to win a wife you must, like old red-head soundly lick
  her,
Course I know you've *wanted* to; but that only works with a
  Miss Woodpicker
Can you imagine how you'd look, like a turkey gobbler struttin',
To pay for pancakes, lovin' up, an' a neatly sewed on button?
Don't you think that you'd feel great, like an old drake quackin',
Or like a guinea in the grass, a floppin' an' pot-rackin'?
When you watch these feathered males, an' their sufferin' mates
  endurin'
Ain't you glad you got a way, more graceful an' allurin'?

           'Gene Stratton Porter.

A Confession

I don't like radishes—one bit me once.

          Mme. Qui Vive.

A Memory Page

Three Women in a Garden

SUNLIGHT glints through wind blown leaves. The scent of mignonette and Summer is in the air.

Said she of the slate-gray eyes—eyes that darkened and lightened, eyes that were sometimes dark as midnight skies and sometimes steely as the sun at noonday—"If he whom I love were false to me I could not find it in my heart to forgive. I must have all or nothing," and the eyes were gray as storm clouds.

Said she of the dark brown eyes—eyes that looked out on life with a look of long-ago pain not yet forgotten—eyes that questioned life, unanswered—"Forgiveness is not impossible, it is the forgetting that is hard. The woman of a man's heart may not always be the woman of his arms—but it is hard to forget—" and the eyes glowed fiercely for a moment at variance with the placid brow.

Said she of the deep blue eyes—eyes like faded violets—eyes that had seen life and now gave forth a benediction—"Women must be the mothers of men's souls. Love is the act of taking in one's youth, of giving in one's middle age and of accepting as the years go by. Forgiveness and forgetting slip from the mind and heart—there is only room at the end for faith—" and the sweetness of much loving, many forgivings and all the forgettings glowed like a flaming candle still burning in the heart.

There was no word spoken. The wind brought the scent of mignonette. A bee buzzed dreamily. A bird murmured soft warnings to her mate.

Elizabeth Curtiss Nolan

Woman

A MAN to whom I was talking, not long ago, said, "Well, if women don't like the laws they have only themselves to blame; they were napping, and men made laws to suit themselves."

Woman "napping," indeed!

She was stunned. Man slugged her over the head and dragged her off—that was the way he got her, originally, and when she came to she was minding the baby with one hand and skinning a deer with the other. A fine chance *she* had to make laws, or even to think about them.

In the prehistoric days man's business in life was to keep himself; his mate, and his offspring alive. As he was the stronger, physically, the getting and keeping of whatever the family had devolved upon him. Might made right. He fought, killed, and stole, that they might exist.

But there was a gentler side to life, even in the old, old days.

As time went on, if the family was to have anything but raw material, the woman had to provide it. She dug up the ground with a crooked stick, she sowed the seed, she reaped the harvests, she ground the meal, she baked the bread to nourish the sons that she bore. She raised the flax to make the fine linen in which to clothe her household. She sheared the lambs, and spun and dyed the wool from which she wove the scarlet cloth in which her lord went forth to sit in the seats of the mighty and to join in the councils of the wise and great. And if, perchance, she were allowed to speak when her master returned to the home which she had made, she gave him of the thoughts that had crystallized in her mind in the long hours of her lonely toil. She softly bade him to remember mercy, to love peace—that righteousness is the mother of all good, of all prosperity, of all happiness—and she pointed the way toward God.

"She had done what she could."

Héloise Wynne.

The Crumpled Rose Leaf

DID you ever hear of that king of old
   Whose chief delight was to fuss and scold,
     And who swore that his bed was so full of humps
That he could not sleep because of the lumps?
Well, on looking to find what the cause might be,
What do you think the maids did see?
Not a piece of wood, nor a chunk of lead,
Nor a ball of yarn, nor a spool of thread,
But just a rose leaf, crumpled and sweet,
Which had clung to the hem of the 'broidered sheet
When drawn from the chest, where in soft repose
It had gathered the fragrance of many a rose.
Just a crumpled rose leaf—that was all!
Yet even this dainty thing, so small,
Could make his worries and frettings double
To this man who wanted to borrow trouble.
And all of us worry and lose our sleep
Over little things, that we hug and keep
Till they grow and grow, and seem to be
High as the hills, and deep as the sea.
Little troubles and little cares,
Wrinkle our faces and whiten our hairs;
Make us fretful and crabbed and old;
Banish our friends, make love grow cold;
And when real trouble at last walks in,
We've no strength left to fight him and win.
Don't waste your life in this foolish way,
Hunting up something by night and day,
That you imagine is going wrong
And you must right it. Just travel along
And try to gather the sweets of life,
Forgetting its sorrows and toil and strife.
Brace up! don't falter and stumble and fall,
It may be but a rose leaf, after all!

Sallie M. Moses.

A Memory Page

An Answer to Kipling's Poem

"The Female of the Species is More Deadly than the Male"

FOR the female of the species is more deadly than the
  male,"
  Is the battle cry of Kipling, in his egotistic tale,
Which decries, O! shame to say it, the sex that gave him birth,
And likens all of womankind to reptiles of the earth;
Wondrous facts he has omitted in his poetic lore;
'Tis strange he has forgotten how heavy women score;
After eating fruit forbidden, Adam tried to lay the blame
On the woman God had given, and it's ever been the same.
Only God and all his angels know the cross the women bear
When they give up happy girlhood for matrimony's care,
Bravely fighting and defeating woes in life that make her quail,
"For the female of the species is more deadly than the male."

There's a woman's name that's sacred, praises sung in every
  tongue,
For she gave mankind a Savior in her own beloved Son;
Inherent, noble Mary, she endowed her child with grace,
The perfect man and master, the Redeemer of his race.
'Twas a woman's instigation sent Columbus o'er the sea,
'Twas a woman's powerful book that helped the negro free;
In the mighty throes of battle, near the thickest of the fray,
'Twas a woman's hand that succored the wounded as they lay
Torn and bleeding, life fast ebbing, one last message home to
  send,
It was given and transmitted by the dying soldier's friend.
No fear had she of shot or shell that showered her like hail,
"For the female of the species is more deadly than the male."

Thus down through all the ages women ever face the fight,
Strong in courage, faith and justice, with her face toward the
  light;
Oft disheartened, often weary, plodding onward brave and
  true,
Ever giving, ne'er receiving, shirking naught she has to do,
She it is who molds the Nation, gives the world her men of
  fame;
She is not a beast of burden—give her credit in her name
For her progress and her virtues—it has been a bitter fight,
For men all through the ages have denied the woman's right
To use the brains God gave her as well as bear men's sons;
For the good of all humanity before life's race is run
She'll solve the many problems, you'll never see her fail,
"For the female of the species is more deadly than the male."

Estelle Ryan Snyder.

Excerpt from "Teaching and Nursing"

HU'MANITY always understands humanity. Races, ages, individuals misunderstand and impede one another.

Indeed, so dulled do we become by tradition perpetuated from accumulated interference with Nature, that we come to accept involved and toggled-up human relations as inevitable, and it does not occur to us that we may rid ourselves of this incubus by opening the springs of human nature and permitting the free forces of Eternal Nature herself to pour through us, into society, her remedial vitality. I say "it never *occurs* to us," for it is rather a need of *enlightenment* than a need of faith which deters us from developing as the lilies of the field do.

Faith every living organism possesses, but, as with all other factors of human activity, it is, as yet, conscious in the few only. Jesus was so conscious an exponent of faith, the simplicity which He brought into all phases of life which He entered was so healing, that His teaching and healing influence has carried through the increasing complexities of two thousand years, and clears the troubled hearts and minds of men today.

It is the *"considering"* that we need.

Nature's laws are always operating, and our Being has faith in them whatever may be the befogged and entangled condition of our minds, which have been led into strange devices. Nature, in turn, has large faith in her novitiate child, trusting to his unconscious Being to fulfill in time normality for the race, while his conscious mind, during its period of initiative, busily sets to work to bewilder human relations into an artificial and crucifying interdependence, which it calls "civilization."

Civilization, as it has been understood, and as we now understand it, is, we suppose, a part of Nature's patient plan. But that it is not the adequate expression of that plan we are inspired to believe every time we consider the lilies of the field.

Cornelia B. de Bey, M. D.

When Carrie Jacobs Bond Sings

WHEN Carrie Jacobs Bond sings
What do we hear and see?
A sweet-brier hedge; waving wings—
Bird, butterfly and bee;
A meadow-lark in daisied field;
A robin at top of white birch tree,
A swinging and singing to you and me,
Of love and trust and joy, and peace,
Of duty and beauty and service and rest—
And the sky is aglow in the west;
A pond-lily pool, a violet bed,
A sorrowing mother with low-bow'd head;
A winding river which sings and purls
As on it travels in eddies and swirls
To join the ceaseless ocean;
The tiny tinkle a wind-harp sings;
The human moaning of violin strings;
The hope and faith of each human heart;
The pain and yearning when lovers part;
A wild-rose thicket where thrushes meet;
A new-made grave in God's acre sweet;—
So many sweet, indescribable things
We see and hear when this woman sings.

Mary Badollet Powell.

Feminine Philosophy

COMMON sense is a commendable quality. It keeps us from doing many foolish acts and it is altogether reliable, like a good kitchen range or a favorite cake recipe. But the trouble with an excess of common sense is that it often crowds out much that is delightfully absurd, beautifully sweet, and tenderly delirious. Also, too much common sense makes us too serious and to be too serious is not to be companionable to those who love us. Beware, you wise ones, lest you grow too wise. A little nonsense—you know the rest.

To allow oneself to be trampled upon is not meekness. It is mere passivity and inertia. A meekness which endures in order that it may shape things better is the real virtue. The gentlest of mothers and wives is often the firmest and most influential. Meekness is not an end but a means to an end. The power of a great anger may lie behind it, and actually enhance its value.

It ought not be a weak attribute of goodness, but a token of strength, self-controlled and dedicated to the service of others. Militant meekness is one of the strongest forces in the world—and no modern woman who expects to accomplish anything should be without it.

Mary Eleanor O'Donnell.

The Wind Some Day

THE Wind some day—the ranting Wind and idle—
  My servitor shall be
    To waft from Fire's caress the dust that mantled
My earth necessity.
That no cold grave cell may, enclosing, stifle
My residue of clay,·
Swift to my need, in answer to the spirit,
From far—in haste—shall come, the Wind some day.
Some day the Wind—that bloweth where it listeth —
A tryst with me shall make.
One last embrace when, dust to dust returning,
Earth's temple I forsake.
Back to the void from which all law was fashioned
The Thinker to obey,
Unparticled, dissolved, from form to freedom,
My liberation waits the Wind some day.

Anstiss C. Gary.

❦

Consecration

CATHEDRAL spire and lofty architrave,
  Nor priestly rites and humble reverence,
    Nor costly fires of myrrh and frankincense
May give the consecration that we crave;
Upon the shore where tides forever lave
With grateful coolness on the fevered sense;
Where passion grows to silence, rapt, intense,
There waits the chrismal fountain of the wave.

By rock-hewn altars where is said no word,
Save by the deep that calleth unto deep,
While organ tones of sea resound above;
The truth of truths our inmost souls have heard,
And in our hearts communion wine we keep,
For He, Himself hath said it—"God is Love."

Myrtle Reed.

The Joys of Gardens

AS NATURE is the Vicar of God, the true Gardener is of the Temple. Many kneel at the altars, their senses enthralled by the incense, the music, the vision of the enthroned cross and the mystical ceremonial, and go away asking, "What does it mean?"

But for the true Gardener every place is a temple, and the arching heavens above the open fields is the greatest vaulted roof of all. He may prostrate himself amid the smoke of sacrifice in cathedral splendor, while his open soul knowing that these are but symbols, takes flight into infinite spaces with longing for a knowledge of the angelic choirs, and one glimpse of Him the source of light and life.

For the Gardener is ever in the company of the invisible Deity. Going hand in hand with Nature, witnessing the hourly miracles of creation, his faith is perennial, his hope renewed, and his conviction firm that there is no death, but that man like the flower transmits life from season to season, plays his part in the immeasurable plan and may rejoice in immortality in the infinite years, which no human mind has yet been able to understand.

Then blest is he who loves and tends a single plant. He is a partner in the mystery, he too may feel the heart of Nature throbbing in the earth. No common joys are his. His thoughts range in the azure skies by day and night, he delights in sunshine and is patient in rain, he never ceases to wonder at the marvel of the lily or the rose, or the commonwealth of grasses in the fields. His companions are the bees, the butterflies and singing birds, and the earth is illumined with celestial light.

Ever with Nature the Vicar of God, the Gardener is never alone. He is conscious of the supreme benediction that falls on those who would make the earth more beautiful by their labors, and so take part in the scheme of the Creator of it all. Forgetful of selfish ends, not seeking ephemeral wealth nor knowledge, the humble Gardener is yet the citizen of the world. His chosen friends of field and garden meet him in mountains, plains or city yards, and so divinely blest he asks no more, but that he may walk with angels in his garden.

Lena N. McCauley.

UP   TO HER

MY Mother's at the Press
      Club—
(She   writes—y' understand).
My Father—he's an artist—
C'n paint to beat the band.

I ain't a bit artistic—
I couldn't write a book—
But some one in this family
'S got to learn to cook.

       Violet Moore Higgins.

The Prince O' The Green World

THE Prince of the Rainbow slid down to earth on a sun thread. The green world, if you must know, O, Alice and Carolyn and Bob so mischief-wise, is a place where something is always fighting to be on top. Sometimes it is Mist o' Rain, and it depends upon the kind of eyes people have as to how they feel on the days she is in power. Sometimes it is Burning Shine, and again it depends on whether people's eyes are strong as to how they feel on his days.

When the little fellow alighted on the grass where the violet's breath made the earth sweet, he found himself at the foot of a tall, slender tree, that wept softly.

"Why do you weep so?" asked the fairy prince.

"On account of the day," sobbed the tree. "Who could be glad in a green world ruled by Mist o' Rain? You have been away a long time," he continued.

"I came to conquer the green world again," answered the Prince of the Rainbow. "I was afraid I should be forgotten and to be forgotten is to cease to live, and I will not die. I must not, for my only existence is in the hearts of the people of the green world, and all hearts would wither without me."

"Oh, I do not know about that," said the sad tree. "There are those who think that nothing is but what one thinks, and there are others who believe that nothing is but what it is possible to touch, and in the green world there are more of the latter. They won't believe in you, so you will cease to exist in a short time in the green world.

"And what do you believe?" asked the Prince of the Sad Tree.

"I?" said the tree. "Well, I do not believe in you at all. What's the use of believing in anything when the green world is in the power of Mist o' Rain? And anyway, I have to hunt so hard and look so far to see you that my neck actually grows painful from the twisting. I don't believe there is any joy, therefore there can be no joy. O, you will soon cease to be in the green world. I advise you to go back to the thought-land on your sun thread and stay there."

The poor Prince of the Rainbow was very much frightened. "I shall die," he thought, "and then the hearts of all living things in the green world will become withered and old and useless, and only powers like Mist o' Rain will visit the green world! O, surely, every one does not believe as you do, great tree!" he cried.

"Every one but the children," replied the sad tree; "and they may soon. One never knows."

"I must find the children quickly!" he cried. He smiled such a gay smile at the thought that a sun thread darted in among the grasses. The prince caught it and on it dipped and soared to all the little children of the green world. "Lend me your smiles!" he called to them, and they all gave them gladly, without question, because the prince was in their hearts.

Then the Prince of the Rainbow took the smiles of the little children and blew them gently through the tear drops of Mist o' Rain and there was reflected such joy of all living things in the green world that a rainbow visited the sky again as a herald, then faded into the glory of the sun.

The Prince of the Rainbow was sure of his life again!

Ruth Kerfoot.

❧

Self Reliance

LITTLE yaller blossom,
　　Peekin' fru de grass,
　　Waitin' mity patient
Foh de storms tu pass.
Goes a-head er smilin',
　　Brighter ebbery day,
Jess keeps on er growin'
　　'Neath skies cold en gray.
Little yaller blossom,
　　If de truf wuz known,
You're jess er makin'
　　Sunshine of your own.

Ophelia Lawrence Blair.

A Hallowe'en Fancy

WHERE are the fairies of yesteryear?
Where are the tender, unseen presences that whole nations once loved?

Hallowe'en is here again.

It's cold without you.

Where is merry Robin Goodfellow, and where is Puck? The pixies, elves and kelpies, where are they? Where is Ariel flown, and where are "the little people"?

> "Wee folk, good folk,
> Trooping all together
> Green jacket, red cap,
> And white owl's feather?"

Where are the little mountain men Rip Van Winkle met in our own Catskills, and where the gnomes of Germany's jeweled mines and mountains?

Where the woodsprites and dryads, the fauns and satyrs of a younger Europe? Where is Daphne? Where is Undine?

Where are the trees that talked, the stones and semblances that were transmuted into beings in a twinkling before believing eyes?

Where are the sprites that put dewdrops in the flowers o' early morn and the sandman that sowed the seeds of sleep?

Gentle dreamful deities of an older world, where have you fled?

Come back! It's Hallowe'en and the world wants you! It wants you more than ever it wanted anything else in all its heavy round, wants the mystery, the tender fear and fearful faith that went away when you went—wants its fairy godmother back; wants its Lorelei, wants its dryads and its Ceres, wants its faith in all beautiful, mystical things.

We thought to stand alone, conquerors of earth!

We prided ourselves on freedom!

You were superstitions and nothing more, we said. You never peopled woods and fields, we mocked. No gods come down from starry skies to brother with mankind.

This was sea and this was land; this a tree and that a rock. There were no Poseidons, no earth-shaking Atlases, no fairy folk, no gods, no goblins!

What have we got in exchange for faith that saw God in every form of nature, Christ in the beggar fed at eve at the woodman's table, the traveler ferried on Christopher's back across the stream?

Night has come upon us, O little people!

A sky without a star is over us.

We are afraid.

O invisible presence of Earth's youth, of reverence and belief and prayer, return, we pray!

The world is cold without you.

It's Hallowe'en!

Mary O'Connor Newell.

44

6

Great Day of God.

Words & Music by L. R. WAITE.

Great day of God, long looked for, Thy dawn we do pro-
Great day of Might and Pow-er, Of Know-ledge and of

claim.Great day when ev-'ry na-tion Shall praise His ho-ly name,Great
Light, No clouds of su-per-sti-tion Can now be-dim our sight,Great

day of re-sur-rec-tion, Of un-i-ty and love, Soon
Day, when God,the Fa-ther, Is known o'er all the earth, And

bright in all its splen-dor Thy Sun shall shine a-bove.
to His whole cre-a-tion Hath giv-en a new birth.

Great Day of the unveiling
Of Truth's Deep mysteries,
When every hidden secret
Of earth and sky and seas,
In all their wondrous beauty,
To man shall be revealed;
Nor can an act or motive
By man now be concealed.

Great Day of God, All glorious;
Great Day of Peace, so blest;
The thought of Thee brings gladness,
And dilates every breast.
Great Day of one religion,
When all are understood;
One faith in Life Eternal,
One God, one Brotherhood.

The Aristocracy of Brains

TELL me who that shabby-looking little woman is over there in that group of stunningly gowned women by the fireplace? How pathetic her poor little hat and gloves are, and doesn't her dress remind you of a rag-bag? She must have sublime courage to come here in that costume, and yet I remember now that I have seen her at all the most elegant functions this winter, and she seems popular, too. How do you suppose she manages it?"

The other woman smiled patiently as she answered: "Why, with her brains, of course. She hasn't any money, so she can't win attention with her clothes or entertaining, and as her people all died before she came here, a stranger, to live, she has not had any family to back her. What little beauty she ever had faded long ago, but she has made herself a personality by using her brains and will power. She has been clever enough to surround herself with brainy people, to be on the intellectual, progressive and uplifting side of every important movement. She is president of our best Woman's Club, and is virtually the head of another prominent organization. She has great executive ability, is clear sighted enough to see the result of anything before it is started, has the wisdom to let go as well as to take hold of the handles of Life's wheelbarrow. She does not use her brains in a cold, calculating, selfish way, but for the attainment of rare culture, love of humanity and fidelity to ideals."

Three friends were motoring home from a reception and the conversation, becoming intimate, turned toward their hostess.

"She doesn't look a day over thirty-five," began one of the women, "and I know she is twenty years older than that. Really, I never have seen her when she looked her age by a dozen years. Of course, she has some gray hairs and one or two characteristic lines, but she always expresses eternal youth to me. What can be her secret?"

"Oh, that is easy," answered another woman; "she hasn't any worries, with a comfortable income, an adoring, congenial husband, no children; what cares or responsibilities has she to age her?"

"Well," said the first speaker, "things, after all, are pretty evenly divided in this world, and you can't tell me that a woman can reach fifty years without sorrows and disappointments."

"You are right," interrupted the third woman, who loved the one they were discussing; "she has had them, too; known what it was to lie awake long, anxious hours in the night, learned to laugh and talk while a grim spectre mocked close behind her; her heart has paid grief and sorrow their usual toll. She had kept young through it all by a life of intense mental activity.

"Her intellectual pleasures and mental activity have helped her forget the cares that could have pressed heavily—the grief that might have corroded—and have left her spirit young, her eyes bright, her entire being responsive, alive, sympathetic and interesting."

Florence Adams Gebhardt.

❧

The Alchemist

UNDER the argentine glow of the Easter-time
We loosen our hold on all sordid conventions
And fling our souls out in the freedom of gladness!
The in-rushing thoughts come sanctioned by joy—
That luring protagonist we eagerly follow.
In the thrill of new life all fear is cast out;
Our listening minds hear the low call of beauty;
The ambient air with the odor of springtime
Is sensuous—the throbbing pulse of Ceres we feel;
The old "immortal indolence" bathes us once more,
And we know we are one with the great Primal Cause.
It is Love has relumed our stifled convictions,
And Love that is rolling the stone away
To give us this opulent Life today.

Pauline Leavens.

A Woman's Thoughts

LOVE is that which makes the State of Matrimony hard to live in unless it is the Capital.

Some women pray for things they'd never dream of working for—husbands included.

The first family separation on record—Adam and his spare rib.

Some girls' complexions are so clear they can be seen through at one glance.

Some members of the oldest families look every day of it.

"When Dreams Come True"—When a spinster takes an upper berth and finds a man under her bed.

Precautionary measures are just as necessary to keeping freckles off your reputation as off your face.

If there's one thing makes a woman madder than to be "ogled" it is not to be noticed at all.

Doris Blake.

Excerpt

AND the White Lady heard a voice within which said: "And he just can't help being 'black' either. Have you ever stopped to think how lucky you are that the Accident of Birth allowed you to be born 'white,' in the big house on your mother's plantation, instead of putting your soul into one of the 'black' skins in a cabin?"

Betty Barlow.

A Dream of Long Ago

THE skies are blue as the skies of June
   Have ever a right to be,
    And my heart is singing an old love tune,
  Pitched to a minor key.
I'm dreaming a dream of olden days
  When life was bright and fair.
Only a dream of a dreamer, dear,
  But I wonder if you would care.

We walk again in the flowery lane,
  Hand in hand as in days of yore.
On the old church tower, on the leafy bower
  The moonlight falls once more.
I listen again to your words of love,
  With rapture beyond compare.
Only the dream of a dreamer, dear,
  But I wonder if you would care.

The wild rose blooming by the hedge,
  Grows pale 'neath the glittering stars.
Heaven whispers low to the waiting earth,
  As we stand at the meadow bars.
I look once more in your love-lit eyes,
  The old fond smile you wear.
Only the dream of a dreamer, dear,
  But I wonder if you would care.

The sound of your voice comes back to me,
  Across the bridge of the years.
My heart is an island standing alone
  In the midst of a sea of tears.
I cover with kisses a faded rose,
  The one you asked me to wear.
Only the dream of a dreamer, dear,
  But I wonder if you would care.

Does the blue of the sky, the breath of a rose,
  A song heard half asleep,
Bring back the past in a sudden rush
  Of feeling strong and deep?
'Twere sweet to think that you and I
  The thoughts of the past still share.
Only the dream of a dreamer, dear,
  But I wonder if you would care.

                Grace Scofield Holmer.

A Japanese Mother

GRAY Choturo heard the tramp
    Of the feet that marched to battle,
    Heard the horses neigh and stamp,
    Creak of belt and side-arms rattle,
Heard the sudden rapt'rous cry:
"Dai Nippon! Banzai! Banzai!"

Near her pillow stayed her son,
And she pressed his shoulder, harking,
When a gun told to a gun
That the soldiers were embarking;
And she heard his heart beat fast
While the countless columns passed.

Proudly looked she in his face—
None who marched without had bolder—
And she drew aside apace,
Leaned more lightly on his shoulder.
Gleam of musket, clink of spur,
Clang of sword, came in to her.

Then she questioned, eye to eye:
"Why art thou not with the others
Where the red-orbed banners fly?
Must I be the scorn of mothers?
Shall I send no son to war
For his gods and Emperor?"

But he smiled: "With thee I stay,
August mother, moon-white lady;
Scorching is the sun of day,
And thy shoji cool and shady."
But she shook her aged head:
"Empty are thy words," she said.

Then he cried: "I stay with thee!
None remain thy life to cherish.
When the war-drums call to me
Can I leave thee here to perish?
By the gods! while thou dost live
All my days to thee I'll give!"

In Choturo's fervent gaze
Land and mother-love were blended!
Then he saw her hand upraise
With a dagger that descended!
And he caught her thrilling sigh:
"Dai Nippon! Banzai! Banzai!"

To his open arms she swayed,
Her kimono crimson turning;
But she laughed and drew the blade
From the breast that ceased its burning;
Gave it to his hand, and so,
Smiling, dying, whispered: "Go!"

Then he laid her gently down,
Smoothed her robe, and left her straightway:
Staggered, stumbled, through the town;
Joined the troops that passed the gateway,
Crying, the red blade on high:
"Dai Nippon! Banzai! Banzai!"

Grace Duffie Boylan.

To Music

IMMORTAL music!
Heav'n's own gift that doth the
souls of men uplift,
Interpreter of all our moods,
Oh, vibrant voice from solitudes,
And cadence tender and sublime,
Oh, linger with us for all time,
In melody, in melody.

Whene'er our souls droop and repine,
Let Music charm with power divine,
If e'er our hearts faint from defeat,
Let Music cheer with rhythmic beat,
Let Music charm with power divine!

Grace T. Hadley.

A Sketch

WHY does the mind retain vividly certain memories when others that would seem to have a vital relation to one's life are recalled only by an effort of the will?

These three pictures recur insistently:

A long stretch of road in late September; a hint of storm; a camp fire and figures in silhouette; suddenly, gypsies at our horses' heads; a hag's face thrust in ours and my opulent companion's hand seized; she snatches it away and says furiously, "My life is behind me—there is nothing you can tell me."

A white moon in the Blue Ridge country; dusky figures grouped under magnolia trees and negro voices singing—"Mah Madeline"—

A river bank; a row boat in tow; still figures under a blanket, their boyish outlines revealed; two pairs of shoes tied together by the strings; a brown paper parcel of lunch. A wisp of towsled hair sticking from beneath the blanket; a woman sobbing wildly as the boat is slowly drawn upon the shore.

Florence Seyler Thompson.

The Shining Mark

THE little red devil unfolded his morning paper and held it in one hand while he toasted his bread on the end of a long fork over the fire. All of a sudden, he dropped the fork, accidentally upsetting his breakfast cup of brimstone, and doubled up with laughter, rolling over and over on the floor in fiendish glee. Then he sprang up and ran to the 'phone.

"Hello Central, give me Death—yes Death. You know the number, I've called it often enough. Hello—this you, Old-timer? Congratulations, old boy. Now don't play innocent; cut the funeral tone. Leave that for the mourners, they may be sincere, you old hypocrite. Your sob stuff doesn't go with me, you old wolf in sheep's clothing. Everybody knows me for what I am. They smell the sulphur, but look what you get away with, mystery, solemnity, Providential dealings, these are the thoughts the poor humans associate with your awesome presence. They think of me as a very malicious creature, but I only go after the bad ones while you, you voracious old bag of bones, you have no mercy. Innocent childhood, youth, early manhood, the great author, the man of affairs, the mother of a family—it's all the same to you. A shining mark—you sure got one this time, didn't you? Stow the voice, mate, it does'nt go with me. Why you can't even cover up your grinning old teeth, so don't get maudlin. A multi-millionaire—some shining mark believe me. And he can't take an ounce of all that metal with him, except the metallic casket. How he worked and slaved for the money— how he worked everybody else for it! Can't you see him climbing up and up that towering pinnacle of gold, on and on over the bodies and souls of men and women and children, wiping out fortunes that his own pile might grow into a glittering mass for fools to gape at, a mountain whose peaks are unattainable to the common herd? And what a write-up they gave him! A philanthropist—one who endowed schools and charitable institutions—a public-spirited gentleman, if you please! I've laughed my sides sore with the farce of it. Oh this isn't all your funeral, old top. I'll have a share in this, I'm thinking. What? You'll concede me the brigand with the black mask and revolver? Thanks. I can see you virtuously drawing that ragged old robe of yours around your unsightly frame. It don't go; I'm wise to you, pard. That hold-up man is a saint from heaven compared with your, I mean our, ex-philanthropist. Blood money—the hoary-headed old pirate—why blood drips from every ounce of his gold! You haven't put anything over me this time, friend, dear friend. Still have the grieved tone? Well, that's part of your stock in trade. I'm going to ring off. now. By-by. Just remember I'm wise. Ta ta."

The little red devil put up the receiver, dancing up and down in his glee and laughing, "Ho! Ho! Ha! Ha!" after the manner of little red devils, which was most sacrilegious, infernal and brimstonic, but then that's all one could expect of a demon of any color, and at least he wasn't a hypocrite, which is saying something.

Mary Moncure Parker.

A Memory Page

Blight and Bloom

LIFE hath its barren years,
  Where fair blooms fall untimely down;
  When ripened fruitage fails to crown
The summer toil; when nature's frown
    Looks only on our tears.

Life hath its faithless days—
The golden promise of the morn,
That seemed for light and gladness born,
Meant only noontide wreck and scorn,
    Hushed harp instead of praise.

Life hath its valleys too,
Where we must walk in vain regret,
With mourning clothed, with wild rain wet—
Toward sunlit hopes that soon must set,
    All quenched in pitying dew.

Life hath its harvest moons,
Its tasselled corn and purple-weighted vine;
Its gathered sheaves of grain, and blessed sign
Of plenteous ripening bread, and pure, rich wine,
    Full hearts for harvest tunes.

Life hath its hopes fulfilled;
Its glad fruitions, its bless't answered prayer,
Sweeter for waiting long, whose holy air,
Indrawn to silent souls, breathes forth in rare,
    Grand speech by joy distilled.

Life hath its Tabor heights;
Its lofty mounts of heavenly recognition,
Whose unveiled glories flash to earth, munition
Of love and truth illumining intuition.
    Hail! mount of all delight.

                    Isadore Gilbert Jeffery.

To the New Woman

LET us drink, then, to the woman of today, and pledge her our good will and support; otherwise she may achieve, unaided and alone, a success whose far-reaching effect can only be conjectured. I refer to the crusade that has for its ultimate goal universal peace and love. With telescopic vision woman has discerned these two stars struggling on the edge of the horizon and she has determined that they shall rise higher and higher in the firmament until they shine resplendent at the zenith. Already her hand is on the charter of human liberties, and she is writing a new gospel of comradeship—a gospel of that better civilization, where husband and wife, brother and sister, work together for the common good of all.

Anna D. Fishback.

Out of the Spice Box

ONE doesn't mind the climbers so much—it's the pushers that set one's teeth on edge.

Poor relatives will vanish when women get all the political jobs—even Uncle John's sister's cousin will get a place then.

Paint is a lot better preservative for old lumber than for girls' faces.

The bachelor girl next door says she is more a believer in double than single tax.

Love is free, but it takes a little money to go to housekeeping.

Don't rely too much on a pair of honest eyes. Some people can teach tricks even to their eyes.

It takes one's home folks to find out and fully appreciate one's faults and mistakes.

There ought to be a special punishment devised for the leeches on your time and wits.

Addie Farrar.

The Mystery Seed

I FOUND a Mystery-Seed. And a Voice said "Place the Mystery-Seed in the hollow of thy left hand; cover it with thy right hand, thereby making a well of warmth and darkness wherein thy seed may have a home. It will germinate and become transformed into a priceless jewel. Cherish it." I heeded the Voice. I placed the Mystery-Seed within the hollow of my left hand, covered it with my right hand and waited. Again the Voice said: "Open now thy hand, obedient one, and find thy treasure." I raised my right hand, and lo! in the hollow of my left hand I beheld a blazing jewel. Its flashing colors blinded my gaze, and I covered mine eyes from the glory which pierced me from its centre. And I felt it shine through my closed eyes e'en while my hand held down the lids, its light was so brilliant and overpowering. And I trembled with a great joy which sank into my soul. And I was still. Again the Voice spake, strong, sweet, tender and soft: "Child of earth, fear not. Uncover thou thine eyes. The shine of the jewel shall help thee to see." I obeyed the Voice. I was not afraid, but opened mine eyes, and looked once more within the opening Mystery-Seed. Its light was now of opalescent hue, wherein a tiny golden thread or chain led straight to the distant centre, and which the Voice guided me to follow. And mine eyes were not blinded by this light; but there came with it a peace that strengthened my gaze and kept it fixed upon the centre which I was to gain. At times it was lost in translucent glory, yet I knew it was there. So when the golden chain became dim, I waited; and while I waited the Voice whispered: "Be calm. It will shine again for thee, this golden thread, and thou shalt follow. The centre thou shalt fully see with thine open eyes, and shalt not be blinded. Look again, O faithful one." I looked as commanded, and the glories of the centre were before me—glories that no words of earth can limn. And mine eyes were strong and could see. And as I looked the Voice again spake, thrilling my inmost being. It came nearer and clearer, seeming to proceed from the centre, and it said unto me: "Once more I speak, O child of earth! Thou hast heard, thou hast felt, thou hast seen, thus art thrice blessed; this jewel is thine to wear within thy heart, but thou must wear it that all may see its shine; if thou dost not it will fade back into the original Mystery-Seed which thou didst find buried within the sands of time. Wear it, O brave of heart, wear it that its light may shine for all earth's beings.

Charlotte Cecilia Robertson.

Reminiscent

IN our Capitol City there dwelt a maiden with the soul and aspirations of an artist—but struggle and toil as she would, she never could make an original drawing or sketch. At the great Art School the instructor's criticism was ever the same:

"Turn your canvas over, Miss Claraday, and try again."

In a moment of despair she realized that she lacked the lofty inspiration and originality of the true artist—that hers was the talent and patience of the painter who copies the work of others more gifted. She could make her little squares and measurements and produce a marvelous imitation of any picture.

Her inconsiderate fellow-students wounded her gentle heart with their sneering remarks about "a mere copyist." One among them who sympathized and recognized her ability advised her to devote her time and talent to the copying of celebrated pictures.

Through much crucified ambition and soul travail she took Mrs. Kinelsey's advice, and one blessed day when Miss Claraday was at work at her easel a woman, noted for her love of art, her great riches and her many beautiful charities, passed through the Art Gallery. Her attention was arrested by the faithful reproduction of the famous original which hung on the wall near the finished copy.

Mrs. Landen was charmed and asked if it were for sale. Miss Claraday gladly answered "Yes," and Mrs. Landen purchased it.

Years after, three women—an artist, a business woman, and a writer—were in Paris. They had wondered at many old and young students trying to copy the masterpieces of the world. Not one seemed able to catch the color and spirit of the original.

Many times this trio went to the Louvre to look at the perfect Venus and to commune with that wonderful woman whose glance has fascinated the world for so many centuries—the incomparable Mona Lisa. One morning, as they approached the shrine, they saw a woman copying that baffling countenance.

"That is the cleverest copy of a picture I have seen in Europe—it is perfect," said the artist.

The painter turned, and her glad voice rang out:

"My dear Mrs. Kinelsey, when did you come? Oh, it is good to see a dear friend once more!"

The speaker was Miss Claraday, looking happy and prosperous. She had achieved success in her chosen field of art and had reached the goal that so many of her fellow-students were still striving to attain—recognition and a studio in Paris.

Busy and content with her work, we left her, after having tea in her wonderful studio.

Ella R. Thomas Haynie.

'Way Upstairs

MY EYES is almost shuttin' an' I can't hold up my head,
  An' I'm so awful lonesome 'at I wish 'at I was dead—
  'Cause it's night—an' ever'body's havin' fun—down-
    stairs—but me
An' 'ere's company at our house 'at's as dressed up as can be.

My Mama's playin' bridge I guess, wif Dad an' all the rest,
  She must forget she said she loved her little boy the best.
I can hear her talkin' too,—an' laughin' 'way up here!
  Where there's nobody to talk to but my horse an' Teddy
    Bear,—

An' there's great big shadows—movin' sometimes,—on the
    wall!
  An' there might be somethin' comin' thro' the window—
    or the hall,
It's my Mama!—Yes, she's comin'—Just a flyin' too!
  An' she's sayin' when she sees me, "Boy I'd rather be with
    you."

'En she holds my hand an' 'en I say what always makes her
    glad—
  'At I thinks she's just the dearest Mama anybody's had.
'En she tucks me up in bed an' helps me say my prayers,
  An' now she don't care nothin' 'bout the company down
    stairs."

Genevieve Cooney-Porter.

A Memory Page

Corinne Brown—A Tribute

BLESSING and blessed is the one who can, like Corinne Brown, living, lead the way, and, passing on, still point the way. Keenly analytic and full of initiative, masterful and fearless, hers was the power to attract thinkers and enthuse them with those great truths which were life to her. Not with the force of a gentle spring shower, but rather with the force of the penetrating storm. Moth-eaten opinions were dislodged, blown about, and cast aside. New, forcible and powerful principles, the foundation of a broader social and industrial life, principles that promised a new conception of the brotherhood of man, were the articles of faith to this woman of true social service.

She loved justice—that sublime attribute. She was far-seeing—that great psychic quality. She was democratic and in touch with all that concerns human joy and sorrow.

When the full measure of criticism was falling upon the polygamy of the Mormon, unerringly she found the weak spot of his accuser. The viciousness of his own Gentile social system was shown and judgment rendered. In substance she said, "The polygamous Mormon gives to each wife a name, and to each of his children support, and thus fulfills his moral obligations. The Gentile repudiates all save his legal obligation. He is no more self-poised than his Mormon brother, but disclaiming the responsibility of action, spreads commercialized vice and founds children's institutions." So did she find good in a despised civilization and pointed out a great defect in our own social system—a defect that must be met and remedied. The ability to separate truth from falsehood, facts from sophistry; the fearlessness to face results, no matter what; the splendid courage to earnestly work out problems thus presented—all these unite in making the Corinne Brown whom today we especially remember—friend, teacher, sister, comrade.

Amelia M. Prendergast.

Give Me the Heart that is Loving and True

GIVE me the heart that is loving and true
No matter how plain be the face;
'Tis softened, blessed by an inward grace
Like the rose that is jeweled with dew.

Oh, not to know love, is not to live;
Dear heart, it is strength, life, and hope;
No one can measure its breadth or scope,
The most precious gift God has to give!

Laura Jean Libbey.

The Jew to Jesus

O MAN of my own people, I alone
Among these alien ones can know Thy face,
I who have felt the kinship of our race
Burn in me as I sit where they intone
Thy praises—those, who, striving to make known
A god for sacrifice, have missed the grace
Of Thy sweet human meaning in its place,
Thou who are of our blood-bond and our own.

Are we not sharers of Thy Passion? Yea,
In spirit-anguish closely by thy side
We have drained the bitter cup, and, tortured, felt
With Thee the bruising of each heavy welt.
In every land is our Gethsemane,
A thousand times have we been crucified.

Florence Kiper.

Sunshine and Shadow

THERE'S a bit of sunshine gleaming
  Over there,
 While I stand in shadow seeming
  Full of care;
But each flicker of the leaves
And the glow of golden sheaves
  Helps me bear.

Though the darkness seems to thicken
  O'er the land,
There is radiance just beyond me
  At my hand.
When alas! I would come near,
Something ever seems to sear
  Where I stand.

But, thank God, my eyes can see it
  Over there,
And its joyous flush of glory
  Seems a prayer,
That it may my shadow kiss
Change its sadness into bliss,
  Everywhere.

       Caroline Coe.

Synthesis, Where Haltest Thou?

SHE, Synthesis Johnson, married a Canuck, hastily, incontrovertibly. His name was Cyril Whizzer. He was of English persuasion, she was of Swedish Massachusetts ancestry.

Thankful was Synthy that "Cyril" was not "Evlyn Marie" and Cyril was equally rejoiced that Synthy's cognomen wasn't "Rosemary Violet." "Any other bloomin' name would smell just as sweet," sez 'e.

With the coyness of extreme youth, she often dubbed Cyl in the eye with a chunk of mud—spit balls not being always available. That same maidenly bashfulness attended her to the altar; Cylly never had the shadow of a choice, for Syn always "intentioned" to marry the helpless creature anyhow.

Now, from a geometrical, ethical and mathematical viewpoint, was not this twain, made one, eminently qualified to become the eugenic parents of a Whizzer family?

Everybody expected Syn and Cyl's marriage to be a failure; the general public was not disappointed. Being natural born enemies, the course of their true love was an eternal howling skidway. Syn wickedly managed to see Cyl's wheels go 'round, and he, having a duck of a temper, wasn't afraid to show it, either.

Soaring into that spiritual effluvia—that divine afflatus, of both hot and cold air suppurating the atmosphere of Massachusetts exclusively, Synthesis remarked: (she had a scheme of which Cyril had a hunch) "Cyril, my angel-face," said Original Syn to Aboriginal Snarl, "you will not force me to become a weeping widow to get the vote, will you, Cylly? Surely you'll heed my prayer; surely you'll take out your final papers and become a citizen of this great, free country, this country where Patrick Henry said to the English: 'Gimme Liberty or gimme death!' Do you not love me enough to do this simple act of justice for a beseeching woman?"

"Naw, I don't, Missus. Yer getting all the rights now that are good for yer constitution, so quit howlin' fer more. That bally 'votes for women' would make you worse to live with than you are now; you'd be head-o'-the-house with me if I forsook bully hold Hingland fer a wooden nutmeg Yankee. You ain't a voter, nor you ever will be." Thus orating Cyril departed with many strides.

The weeping woman threw herself on her stomach and said

something not fit for publication in Swede, but taking encouragement from the thought of how many votes would be cast out because the women who cast them didn't make their given ages and the year of their births jibe, she arose from the depths and began figuring on an old envelope.

After Cyril's premature taking-off, there only remained the awful alternative of marrying an American to gain her citizenship—and what might she not butt into?

Hark! Cylly's step! He approaches, hands her some papers, says:

"I saw biscuits in your eye, old gal, and I do this to save my life."

Julia Katherine Barnes.

❧

A Message

A NEW-FOUND truth has been given to the world as the result of an "inspiration" to venture upon the bitherto unexplored and almost sacred grounds of the subject of "voice talent." The fallacy or truth of the universally accepted belief that a beautiful singing voice is God-given and a "talent" and hence an attribute of the mind or soul or emotion, we must ascertain; or whether the voice is an attribute of the physical nature and an instrument lying latent within this body of ours, hidden from human sight, gradually becoming diseased and wasting away following the natural course of things in nature to atrophy if not put to natural uses.

The first real discovery made over twenty years ago virtually rang the death knell of the old belief that a beautiful singing voice is "God-given." The hope is extended to all that a beautiful singing voice is the birthright of not a few, but all, of God's children.

Each and all who wish to expend the time and labor to the perfecting of their instrument can sing themselves to perfect health and happiness, and to all those with the inborn talent of the artistic mind, soul and temperament, into perfect health, wealth and fame.

Anna Groff-Bryant.

A Memory Page

A Paradox

WE READ, "Cast all thy care
        Upon the Lord, and He will thee sustain."
    We lay our burdens there
At His dear feet, then take them up again.
    We pray "Thy will be done,"
With white lips "bless His holy name." We sleep
    With tear-wet cheeks, and moan
In troubled dreams; then wake again to weep.
    We read, "Judge not lest ye
Be judged." We calumny repeat, and smile
    In quiet mockery,
Upon the woe that we have wrought, erstwhile.
    On bended knees we pray,
"Good Lord deliver us, our sins forgive."
    We rise and go our way,
The selfsame wayward life again to live.
    Down through the ages' mist,
From Calvary's lone heights, we hear anew
    These low sad words of Christ:
"Forgive them for they know not what they do."

Ada B. Read.

My Baby

YES, you are mine, you little thing of mystery,
        So eerie like you drifted in, with no line of written
            history;
'Twould seem you might be strange to me,
So lately from the Infinite eye;
But yet you know the mother touch
With none to tell you why.
The mother love had yearned for you,
Baby, oh, my baby!
The mother heart had throbbed for you,
Baby, oh, my baby!
We know each other, dear;
The deep, unfathomable look,
That binds my baby's love to me,
Was never writ in book.

Helena Bingham.

Easter

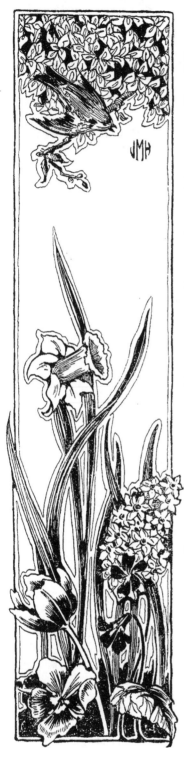

BIRDS twittered, snuggling close. Squirrels scampered madly, scattering with their bushy tails particles of fine, dry snow.

The sun rose from a mist of fleecy clouds, coaxing into beauty dainty snow-drops, their petals glistening like diamonds.

Tiny pieces of the sky had been used to make the cilla so blue! Trees and shrubs hung heavy with tiny, bursting buds. The grass was broken in a thousand places by saucy crocuses that opened wide to greet the new-born day.

Over on the south terrace the air was sweet with the fragrance of violets that called to mind other days of joy and sorrow. Stately hyacinths and dignified narcissi added their wealth of perfume to the air.

In a corner, but where all the world could see, the jonquils and daffodils flung their heads toward the sun and dared the snowflakes to spoil their yellow frocks. A pansy, its purple cloak folded close, shivered in the crisp breeze.

A noisy blue-jay in the oak broke the stillness of the morning and over in the big maple Robin-Redbreast, wooing his mate with a tender love-carol, sung of the beauties of the garden, reminding the world that it was Spring and Resurrection Day.

Jean C. Mowat.

To Sam and Other Boys

GENERAL KNOWLEDGE came riding to town,
　　Astride an arithmetic;
　　　He wore a high hat and a flowing gown,
And carried a great, big stick;
"What, ho!" he shouted, "what, ho, I say,
Where are the girls and the boys?
I'm off for a jaunt and along the way
Are ever so many joys.
The road is all paved with good books for blocks,
The trees hang full of my fruit;
I've keys that fit into all of the locks
Of the houses—built to suit."
But would you believe that the girls and boys
Just turned and all ran away,
And answered: "We don't want to leave our toys;
We'll join you some other day."
Old General Knowledge just shook his head,
"'Tis ever the same," said he;
"But when that day comes I know, instead,
They'll be running after me."
So General Knowledge went on his way,
And I hope if he calls you,
You'll go right along the very same day;
You've found a friend if you do.

　　　　　　　　　Edith Brown Kirkwood.

A Memory Page

Madonna Mary

DIDST look upon thy child as he lay sleeping,
And sigh, "Too fair art thou for this world's keeping,
Too pure to be by sin beguiled;"
Not knowing of the wondrous life before him,
Spotless, holy, undefiled?
Or, did there leap into thy heart this one feeling,
The rarest joy, while thou wert kneeling,
Because a child was born to thee?
Ah! surely thou did feel what all we mothers feel,—
When the firstborn child is placed within our arms, —
Ecstatic, rapturous bliss.
And thou didst press the soft, sweet face against thine own,
And didst print upon the velvet, dewy lips,
Love's holiest, sweetest kiss.
Ah! then did thine eyes grow dim with falling tears,
Ah! then did thy heart beat fast with portent fears.
Then did the hush of silence make dumb thy lips,
And in thine inmost soul thou cried,
"O God, Most High! Of Father of Us All!
Make me fit guardian for Thy sacred trust."

Josephine Turck Baker.

The Rain

IT IS raining here in Kansas,
Crystal drops of hope new-born;
Arid fields, release your incense,
It's in time to save the corn!

There's a growing-song of promise,
Rising from the thirsty grain;
Reaching to the mighty markets,
Governed by this tardy rain.

Prayer is answered in abundance,
Sing Te Deums to the morn;
It is raining here in Kansas,
Just in time to save the corn!

Euretta D. Metcalf.

Mammy

THE color line has never been considered where "mammy" is concerned, for her position in life is clearly defined, and her social position is undeniable. On terms of real intimacy with the best families in the town, because of her faithful service in "givin' rubs," she is sure of a warm greeting, a good meal and liberal compensation wherever she goes.

Then, too, her keen sense of humor makes her a source of enjoyment to the "shut-ins" who look eagerly to her coming and listen with pleasure to her ideas on various topics of the day.

"Her babies," as she always refers to her patrons, range in years from twenty to eighty, and she mothers them all with a real affection, entering into their joys or sorrows with an interest that is genuine.

It is not at all uncommon to see "Mammy" standing complacently on the corner, talking confidentially to one of the most prominent women of the city, waving her hand at another, or riding comfortably in a limousine to the home of one of her patrons.

The community had become accustomed to "Mammy" as a widow, living happily with her family of children, so when she yielded to the ardent wooing of Mr. Johnson—a more than middle-dyed "culled gentleman"—and became Mrs. Johnson, everyone was delighted to think Mammy had found a home and a help-mate.

Alas for her expectations, her hopes were rudely shattered within the first week! "Mistah" Johnson not only proved to be penniless but had a strong disinclination, amounting to positive hatred, for anything that even resembled work. "Misery" in his back served as an excuse for a time, then as the trouble became known and people tried to help Mammy by getting Mr. Johnson some work, he flatly refused to do anything more strenuous than appear at meals.

" 'Help-eat'—that's what I calls him," sighed Mammy as she bought an extra cut of beef, and more groceries. Mistah Johnson grew fatter, and hungrier, and Mammy worked harder than ever, until finally she rebelled and locked him out. He calmly waited till morning on the door-step and appeared with a good appetite for breakfast. She tried again and didn't open the door next time till breakfast was over. Mistah Johnson looked sad, but crept in and waited for dinner.

Finally Mammy grew desperate and made it clear to Mistah Johnson that he must leave permanently. Then she consulted the "Jedge" and in time secured a divorce.

Shortly after this as she was walking up the street with her pail of salt and bottle of oil, Mrs. Jones, one of her "babies," met her and called out: "Well, Mammy! where are you going today?"

"I'se goin' to rub out a di-voce," answered Mammy, her face wreathed in smiles.

"Rub out a divorce!" exclaimed Mrs. Jones. "How on earth can you do that?"

"Easy," chuckled Mammy. "You see, I didn't have no money to get my di-voce from that low-down Johnson, so Jedge Brown he jest got it foh me, and I'se payin' foh it by rubbin' his wife."

Emily Lloyd.

❧

An Ode to Louisiana

OH, my heart's in Louisiana,
    Where the sweet magnolias bloom,
    In the balmy air's Nirvana,
And the sunshine chases gloom.

Where the mocking birds sing sweetly,
    In the moss-draped oak tree grove;
Melting lovers' hearts completely,
    As beneath they fondly rove.

Here the heart is filled with gladness,
    The pulse beats high with joy,
Content am I, for me no sadness
    Can Southland's charm destroy.

Mary Helm.

A Desirable Location

THEY were two Johns who lived in the country. They were grizzled and wrinkled but happy withal, and interested in each other and in things generally.

John No. 1 was driving by on his way to town. John No. 2 stopped him.

"Hey, hitch yer horse and come along; I've got something to show you."

John No. 1 replied, "Be jinks, I'd better be goin' on to get back before dinner."

"Come on, John; come on. I'll hitch fer ye. Stand still, Topsy. Come on, John; 'twon't take but a minute."

John No. 1 straightened out his stiff knee carefully and lumbered down to the ground.

"Hurry up, then, John. Which way?"

"Right through the woods here."

John No. 2 ducked his head and started through the woods, John No. 1 following at his heels.

"Where is it, John?"

"Straight on," said John No. 2, grown taciturn with his approaching triumph.

John No. 1 manfully kept up the pace.

"Are we nearly there?"

"Pert' near."

"How much farther is it, John?"

Suddenly John No. 2 stopped before a low-hanging bush and fell on his knees, pointing and parting its branches.

"There it is."

"What is it?" asked John No. 1, peering.

"Turkey's nest," said John No. 2.

John No. 1 looked closer.

"I don't see any turkey's nest," he said.

"Nice place fer one," said John No. 2.

Edna Herron.

Suffrage Song

COME, let us stand this hour,
   Women with woman's power,
      O'er all this land.
And let the heavens ring,
While we our freedom sing—
Let us our best gifts bring
      To bless our land.

Our leaders bravely fought;
We love the truths they taught
      In Freedom's name.
Shall we less nobly stand,
Daughters of this fair land?
Come, join us hand in hand,
      In Freedom's name.

Oh! hear our children's call.
Wake! hearken! lest they fall
      In Evil's way.
We stand, alone for Right.
Then let us show our might.
Come, help us win the fight,
      This glorious day.

While God we give all praise,
The Stars and Stripes we raise—
      Our country's flag.
Long may it wave above,
Emblem of Truth and Love,
No eagle, but a dove—
      Our blessed flag.

Hattie Sinnard Pashley.

Labor That Endures

AMONG the world of work and workers we so often hear the expression, "When I get rich I won't have to do this work," but never has such sentiment been recorded as coming from the lips of a writer. To the adherent of Thought and Imagination, wealth would not present the means of an escape from labor, but shed the glow of better opportunity for advantages to continue and enhance it. Writing, to the writer, is a life work; it infuses her veins, becomes embedded in her soul, and literary ambition remains the same whether pursuing it handicapped by the demands of necessity, or utilizing wealth to gather gems with which to glorify it. It is this characteristic love of the pen which spurs its following on to the Heights of Fame, and those who reach it continue as earnestly, as diligently, as when on the winding way to the goal, for the writer's effort is *esto perpetua*.

Maybelle Strawbridge.

Maxims of the Business Woman

MIGHT is not right, but right is mighty.

It is not necessary to say all we believe, but it is necessary to believe all we say.

Luck is good, but pluck is better and more to be relied upon.

Sentiment is no substitute for common sense.

To remain unspoiled in prosperity is the test of true character.

To belittle oneself does not raise one in the estimation of others.

We should know not only what we believe, but why.

What you mean to do does not count. It is what you do that makes your record.

It takes courage to wear old clothes and look out of date in order to keep out of debt.

To speak well is good; to think well is better; to do well is best.

Hattie Summerfield.

To A Sleeping Babe

LILY petals and angel wings,
    And all of the delicate, dainty things
        That are sweet, illusive and full of grace
Are found in a sleeping baby's face.

Eleanor L. Drew.

Patience

*"For ye have need of patience, that, after ye have done the
will of God, ye might receive the promise."* (Heb. x:36.)

WE HAVE great need, O weary hand,
    When sunset's gold shall flood the land
        And find your daily task undone,
While evening shadows slowly come;
But rest is here, and rest is thine,
It shall be light at evening time.

Ye have great need, O weary feet,
Whose restless fevered pulses beat
O'er thorny path and rocky height,
In noontide's heat, or starless night;
But on the crystal river's shore
Is peace and rest forever more.

"Rest in the Lord and wait for Him."
Though days be dark and hope be dim,
Through martyr fires with naked feet,
Be loyal still while heart shall beat;
For hope and promise both are thine:
It shall be light at evening time.

Elizabeth A. Reed.

A Memory Page

God's Call to Rest

Underneath are The Everlasting Arms.—Deuteronomy
xxxiii, 27.

THE Sunset's banners fade far down the West.
    Twilight and darkness and the evening star!
    O, soul of mine, heed thou God's call to rest
Sent to thee from the star-strewn heavens afar.

From weary heart and brain loose thou the bands
    That bind thee to thy toil while it is day;
Thy heaven-appointed task leave in His hands
    Who holds the planets on their circling way.

While on thine eyelids dewy pinioned night
    Soft wings shall press, the stars their paths will keep;
The Universe swing softly in the light
    Of Him whose eye doth slumber not nor sleep.

Rest, sleep; entrusting to His Heart of Love
    All cares, all fears, the garish day's alarms;
The dome of heaven thy canopy above,
    And underneath The Everlasting Arms.

Helen Ekin Starrett.

By CAROL KELLEY BROOKE

Random Thoughts

IN THE forgetfulness of self one may accomplish much by lending the helping hand, giving a kindly word or by the sympathetic touch. Thus is the individual like fleecy clouds, ever drifting far apart, yet reaching many.

Have you ever watched a falling star and almost with compassion exclaimed, "Poor little star, you've taken a tumble from your lofty sphere down into an untried world, and you will never shine again! Had you but been content, your brightness and usefulness would have long continued!"

If nature has bestowed upon you a sunny disposition, a true loving heart, then endeavor to gain the daily stimulus of promoting happiness in the lives of others, thereby brightening and strengthening yourself.

"Help one another," a grain of sand said to another grain just at hand. "The wind may carry you over the sea, and then Oh, what will become of me?" "Ah, come my sister, give me your hand; we'll build a mountain and there we'll stand."

Ella L. Plane.

✖

The Book and the Home

NOTHING is so homeless as a bookless house, unless it be a house whose books betray a vulgar and narrow conception of life. A man's books form an average portrait of himself. Without books the merchant's palace becomes but a prison, "the trail of the upholsterer over it all," while a small library, well selected, may, like Aladdin's lamp, turn the abode of poverty into a princely home.

It is a sweet remembrance, that of a quiet old farm-house, where a tired mother after a hard day's work gathered her seven children about her, her knitting-needles keeping time to the measures of the verses read by one of the group from a great poet. The poetry which she knit into the lives of her boys has outlasted all the stockings, and crowned her memory with a halo of poetic recollections.

The boy whose mother "would not go to bed until she had finished reading Pepacton" with him is more to be envied with his poor jacket than the elegant lad whose mother, with no time to read, makes time to consult the latest fashion plates that he may be handsomely attired.

An uneducated working-man, deploring his lack of early advantages, was in the habit of taking his little son on his lap at night to hear his lessons. He followed the boy through all of his high school work, and is today an educated man through giving the child continued sympathy in his studies.

Mary E. Burt.

❧

The Tryst

LOVE, my Love, the sunset splendor
　　Left the world an hour ago;
　　　The maiden moon, all shy and slender,
　　Swooning in the fervid glow.
'Neath curtains drawn, the earth is listing
　　The wooing sibilants of the sea;
O'er land and wave, to keep our trysting,
　　Your constant spirit speeds to me.

Love, my Love! weird fancies thronging,
　　As the south winds crisp the sea;
Joy, misgiving, hope and longing,
　　Have their minor tone for me.
Yours may be God's calm forever,
　　Safe from touch or jar of Fate,
Far as star-sown depths can sever
　　From me, who expect and wait.

Love, my Love! in purple drifting,
　　Summer dusk and valley fills;
To the bending skies uplifting
　　Reverent brows, rise altared hills.
By the meaning hush of even,
　　By the mirrored deep in deep,
By your bourn in earth or heaven,
　　I know our holy tryst you keep!

Marion Harland.

Memory

EXISTENCE has given us a few sublime fabricators like Memory, Poetry and Dr. Cook. They are inaccurate as art and aged pianolas. But we are slaves to their untrustworthiness and find entertainment in their moonshine.

Age accumulates a peculiar fondness for the mental relics that are classified by the psychologists under the name of Memory. Even before one is thirty, Memory becomes a sentimental companion with some other function than those of spelling correctly, hoarding telephone numbers and keeping statistics on the birth rate in France.

It begins to give us those beatific revivals of the past such as are embodied in "The Old Swimmin' Hole," "I Dreamt I Dwelt in Marble Halls," and "The Old Oaken Bucket." It systematically lies to us about our experiences. Its unwritten fiction is as pious a fraud as Chambers' tales of reality.

Besides winning spelling bees and making inaccurate histories, Memory has to its credit a few songs in minor keys, innumerable painful-looking mausoleums and the correct ages of a few of our women friends.

That the use of Memory means retrogression is proven by graduation orations, the drama and political speeches.

Each time one uses his Memory he steps into the past. It is a waste of time. To browse around in the mental debris of a fellow traveler or to learn ancient history are, therefore, putting blocks in the path of progress.

The Moral—Forget it!

Hetty F. Cattell.

A Few Thoughts

THERE is but little unselfish generosity in the world. The saloonkeeper who gives pretzels with his beer, knows the value of salt.

Woman's innocent determination to keep nothing from her husband has resulted only in a reputation for talkativeness.

Some silent people are like country pumps, you can get enough out of them if you keep them well primed.

A great writer has said: "Woman is the greatest work of the Divine Author and every man should own one copy." But this is no excuse for some men trying to own a whole library.

It is foolish to regret that a woman wastes affection on a dog; it is probably no more than a fair valuation.

Mary E. Rae.

The Mutability of Man

WHEN dainty Spring, with sandaled feet,
Comes tripping forth with promise sweet
Of sunshine, flowers and garlands fair,
My heart's enmeshed in golden hair,
I sing of love to eyes of blue.
No other eyes seem half so true.

When Summer's scorching breath I feel
Before another shrine I kneel.
O, sensuous lips and nutbrown hair,
Can other loves with yours compare?
From thee and love I ne'er would stray,
O, soulful eyes of shadowy grey.

When Autumn, saucy, smiling flirt,
In russet gown o'er crimson skirt,
Holds high the brimming goblet filled
With dewy nectar, heaven distilled;
O, eyes of brown, I pledge to thee,
My heart from thine will ne'er be free.

When Winter, radiant, brilliant sprite,
Appears in jewelled robes of white,
My heart's entangled in the net
Of waving, curling locks of jet.
O, eyes of black, thou'rt all to me;
My heaven on earth is found in thee.

Virginia Peyton Campbell.

❧

My Creed

I BELIEVE that all beauty is a gift from God, and that it is given to all women.

I believe that every woman should be beautiful from the cradle to the grave.

I believe that a beautiful physique must contain a broad mind and a sweet spirit of charity.

I believe that beauty of form and feature can be cultivated in every woman until she can be made to "blossom like the rose."

I believe in the sane normal woman who realizes that to live life at its fullest, she must be beautiful, physically, mentally and spiritually.

I believe that the earnest intelligent women of all ages will subscribe to this creed, for as education and culture grow, into the heart of every woman must come a greater desire for the good, the true, and the beautiful.

Lillian Russell.

85

Daybreak

DAY'S approaching from the east,
Heralded by bird and beast,
Seen in lighter, brighter sunbeams climbing up the
golden way.
Lingers in this crimson quiet,
Hint of night's great grief to die at
Just the hour when comes the riot
Of the breaking of the day.

Higher mounts the sun o'er earth,
Dew besprinkled clods give birth
To the breaking, waking seed pods, lifting up a tender blade,
Promise of the harvest coming;
Flow'ring stem with bees a-humming,
Morning's million fingers strumming
Music, while the shadows fade.

Cities wake at daybreak's call,
Slowly lifts the night mist's pall,
Eager workers, shirkers, failures, filling up the broad highway;
Going at the call of duty
Over paths dull, hard and sooty,
With the God-created beauty
Of the breaking of the day.

Salena Sheets Martin.

My Desire

To be able to love my neighbor
and mine enemy as myself
— truthfully, wholly and
wisely;

To believe the best and forget
the worst;

To be honest in my dealings
whether with rogue or wise
man;

To keep within my heart an
ideal which human nature
cannot shatter;

And to be capable of loving
to the end of the chapter,
for love is life.

Frances Armstrong Woods

A Memory Page

The Master Painter

GOD loves the beauty he creates, there lie
    Foam lilled wastes of blue, that clasp the land,
    Caress the rocks, or mingle with the sand,
Shot through with rainbow colors from the sky:
Rivers that flash reflected woodlands by,
Deep, silent pools, where sweet star angels stand,
Imaged through dewy nights, a shining band:
Pearl mountain crowns, that only meet His eye.
Forests of bloom, and shade, man never sees,
Valleys that lapse in sunlight, and in song,
Soft moonlit spaces, melting into air,
Gleaming of dawns and sunsets: all of these
He notes as suns and planets spin along,
And tints with love, His landscapes everywhere.

Emma Playter Seabury.

A Year

ONE more thread in the woof of Time,
    Is woven up and nether,
    Into the nap to overlap
The warp years tie together.

Each day the tint of deeds and thoughts
    Imprinted grave or gaily,
This spotless thread, while heart and head
    Its pattern fashioned daily.

As the shuttle speeds its winding course
    In between the warp of days,
Each tint or shade position made
    To follow the pattern's ways.

Thus weaves and reels each full long year:
    Thus builds of weal and of woe:
With throbbing heart that silent part
    Which ennobles the warp below.

Florence King.

The Children

THE great Pliny once said: "Give me the first seven years of a child's life and you may have the rest, for he is safe."

This is my appeal: the first seven years; give them a chance—train their muscles, train their sense of rhythm, train their breathing. Give them a harmony, give them health—and they will attain purity and happiness.

John, aged seven, lying on a couch, eyes crossed and legs shriveled, laughs through his tears as Charles, aged seven, stands on his head and turns cartwheels for John's amusement.

John has every care. Taught to think only of his chances of being hurt or harmed, through fear cut off from living free.

Charles is alive, having been kept steadily at work fitting himself to fight off the one great bugbear of life—Fear.

Fear rules the world—Fear and Love.

Therefore, I make this plea for the children—give them a chance, until Fear takes to its heels and runs away! Better a cartwheel turned than the cultivated culture pot for the "White Plague." Better the desire to fight the fence-posts with a wooden sword than cross eyes and bandy-legs!

Jean Van Vlissingen.

On Roget's Thesaurus

ON MY desk a Thesaurus lies, old, worn and somewhat faded. My fondness for it only vies with my respect for all its wise arrangement. The words fanfaronnade and foe are only two of many. Without it I would scarcely know the synonym of ápropos or begum. Oh! Dr. Roget, you have saved me many times from trouble. When words refused to come you gave me respite and supplied the grave omission. To you my tuneless voice I raise—'tis pity 'twere no better—in willing songs of heartfelt praise for each elusive word that stays within it.

Lavon Cheney.

Armenian Legends

RMENIA is naturally rich in early legends, the most conspicuous and interesting of which are the bird legends, presumably because the birds of Armenia are countless in number and variety, from the vulture to the wren. An old belief still survives in Armenia that the souls of the blessed dead fly down from heaven in the shape of beautiful birds, and perching on the branches of trees look fondly upon their dear ones as they pass beneath. When in the woods, if a peasant sees birds fluttering about over his head, he will on no account molest them, but will say to his child, "That is the spirit of your dear mother," or "That is your dear little brother," as the case may be. "Be a good child or it will fly away and never again look at you with its sweet little eyes."

ONCE upon a time, when all geese were wild and free, one goose said to another, on the eve of a journey:

"Mind you are ready, my friend, for—please God, I set out tomorrow morning."

"And so will I, whether it pleases God or not," was the irreverent reply.

The next morning both geese were up at daybreak. The religious goose spread his wings and soared lightly toward the distant land, but lo! when the impious goose tried to do likewise, he flapped and flapped but could not stir an inch from the ground. A strolling countryman took possession of him and thus it came about that this irreverent goose and his children fell forever into slavery.

Katherine Wallace Davis

Anecdotes

A WOMAN went to a department store to select a present.

There were about ten people at the book counter, and only one clerk.

Hastily running her hand over the neatly arranged books, she asked, "Is Oliver Twist here?"

"What department does he work in?" was the rejoinder.

::　　::　　::

A country woman recently went into court for the first time. She came home greatly excited.

"Do you know," she said, "the way people are fighting nowadays is something terrible? Why, friend is fighting against friend, and brother against brother. There was the case of Adam against Adam, Brown against Brown, and Jones against Jones. Isn't it awful? It's as bad as the Civil War."

Mary H. Henson.

After the Programme

The congratulation fiend opens the exhaust.

CAN you buy the Marian Bowlan Monologues at the Methodist Book Store?

How old were you when you began to elocute? Reel-y?

Has anybody else composed monologues besides yourself and Browning? (Note the order.)

Are you going into vaudeville? You don't?

Do you look in a mirror when you rehearse those facial expressions?

Don't you just die laughing while you're practising?

Why don't you do something sad? You think you do?

Is "Minnie at the Movies" true?

Could one ever get another costume like your Popular Music Counter Girl's? Not for money?

Don't you think you'll ever go in for tragic acting like Marie Dressler's?

(Business of fainting on the witness stand.)

Marian Bowlan.

A Sylvan Tragedy

THAT fool doctor, he says, "Get away from the noise of the city, Tim, or you'll be a dead man in a month. Sleep in the woods," says he, "with the sky for a roof and the ground for a bed and your sickness 'll fall off like the leaves from a tree."

So I goes, and at dark I fixes my bed under the trees and the sky and mosquito netting. I no sooner gets settled than someone near yells, "Katie did, she did!" and another feller throws back, "Katie didn't, she didn't!"

I didn't give a hang whether Katie did or didn't, but them two keeps it up till a feller off a bit calls, "Who-oo, who-oo?" and somebody answers, "Bob-White! Bob-White!"

Well, I goes to the woods for quiet and have to listen to Katie and Bob White yelling their business out in the middle of the night!

Pretty soon the beggars begins again, "Katie did, she did!" and, "Katie didn't, she didn't!" and then a soft voice sings, "Coo-oo, coo-oo!" making fun of them, and another one cries sharp: "Whip poor Will, Whip poor Will!" What they wants to whip poor Will for when Bob White is up to tricks is more than I can see.

Then the tattle tale begins on Katie again, "Katie did, she did!" and the other objecting, says, "Katie didn't, she didn't!" and the feller that wants to know asks, "Who-oo, who-oo?" and if you'll believe it, the answer this time comes, "Bob-o-Link, Bob-o-Link!" Another feller entirely, by jiggers!

Then, of a sudden, a new voice says solemn like, "Kill-deer, kill-deer," and I hears cry after cry like a hurt cat and I'm certain Bob White or Bob O. Link killed "Dear" on account of Katie.

I starts running and never stops till I hears the purring of the elevated. City noises ain't so bad!

No, I didn't die like the doctor says. I goes fishing on the pier every day for two weeks, and my sickness falls off like the scales from a fish.

Maude Swalm Evans.

The Homeless Scribbles

A SCENARIO

Synopsis:

The Scribbles were a family of two hundred girls. A sad thing about this family was they had no home. To remain united they met occasionally in a cold pillared hotel with a hushed fountain and managed to remember each other's name and age. They longed for a home of their own with an open fireplace to dream beside in winter, and trees and mignonette to waft sweet breezes and fragrance in summer, while true sisterly ties waxed closer around the low tea tables on the veranda. The desire for home consumed them and one day they conceived a brilliant idea—they would write a book, publish it, rake up the proceeds and buy a home. Inspired, palpitating, they went to work. The book was finished, the publisher's obsequies over, and the covers of the Scribbles' struggles throbbed over its scintillating gems. It was a success! The first edition melted away and the sisters stayed up nights to count their money. Real estate men with automobiles filled with radiant Scribbles scurried through the suburbs, until at last the Spot Perfection was found where dreams of the fireplace, mignonette and veranda were to be realized. The Scribbles had a home at last— and lived there happy ever after.

Scene 1.

Fountain room of Hotel. The Scribble Sisters, homeless, despondent. Brilliant Sister Ethel trying to cheer them.

Scene 2.

Cheerless room. Meeting of the Scribble Sisters. An idea strikes them. They decide to write a book and use the proceeds for a home. All inspired, hopeful.

Scene 3.

Same cheerless room. Scribble Sisters counting huge piles of money. Copy of book, a brilliant success, on table. All happy, excited.

Scene 4.

New Home of the Scribbles. Suburbs. Interior. Large living rooms, open fire, small Scribble at piano, others dancing, some sipping tea, some lounging in easy chairs, laughing, chatting. All deliriously happy.

The End.

Roselle Dean.

Roster

Roster—Continued

CPSIA information can be obtained
at www.ICGtesting.com
Printed in the USA
BVHW081601280119
538839BV00027B/2159/P